Introduction to Bitcoin

What is Bitcoin?

Definition and Overview

Bitcoin is a decentralized digital currency, a pioneering form of money that operates without the oversight of a central authority or government. Unlike traditional currencies, Bitcoin exists exclusively in the digital realm, functioning through a global network of computers. It was introduced in 2009 by an individual or group under the pseudonym Satoshi Nakamoto, with the aim of creating a peer-to-peer electronic cash system that could operate securely and autonomously. Bitcoin's foundation is the blockchain, a public ledger that records all transactions transparently and immutably. This innovative approach to currency seeks to solve the issues of trust and intermediation inherent in traditional financial systems.

Key Features

The distinct characteristics of Bitcoin set it apart from conventional currencies and payment methods:

Decentralization: Unlike fiat currencies managed by central banks, Bitcoin operates on a decentralized network of computers. This decentralization ensures that no single entity has control over the currency, enhancing its resistance to censorship and manipulation.

Limited Supply: Bitcoin's total supply is capped at 21 million coins, a feature coded into its algorithm. This scarcity mimics the properties of precious metals like gold and is in stark contrast to fiat currencies, which can be printed indefinitely by governments, leading to inflation.

Divisibility: Bitcoin is highly divisible, with the smallest unit, the "satoshi," representing one hundred millionth of a Bitcoin. This divisibility makes Bitcoin adaptable for transactions of any size, offering flexibility not always feasible with traditional currency units.

Digital Nature: Being entirely digital, Bitcoin transcends physical boundaries, enabling instantaneous global transactions without the need for intermediaries like banks. This digital aspect reduces transaction times and costs, making Bitcoin an efficient medium of exchange.

Uses and Acceptance

Bitcoin's usage has expanded far beyond its initial conception as a peer-to-peer electronic cash system. It now serves multiple functions:

Online Transactions: Bitcoin is widely used for online purchases, offering a high degree of privacy and security. Its borderless nature makes it ideal for international transactions without the hassle of currency conversion or high fees.

Investment: Many view Bitcoin as a digital store of value, akin to digital gold. Its limited supply and increasing acceptance have led to its consideration as an investment asset, with individuals and institutions allocating a portion of their portfolios to Bitcoin.

Retail Purchases: Bitcoin's acceptance in the retail sector is growing, with businesses worldwide starting to accept it as payment for goods and services. This trend is facilitated by payment processors that convert Bitcoin to fiat currency, reducing the risk of price volatility for merchants.

Bitcoin vs. Traditional Money

Bitcoin presents a novel alternative to traditional fiat currencies through its unique features:

Decentralization: The decentralized nature of Bitcoin means it operates without the need for a central authority, reducing the risk of manipulation and censorship that can occur with fiat currencies controlled by governments and central banks.

Control and Ownership: Bitcoin gives users full control over their funds, with transactions being irreversible without the consent of the recipient. This contrasts with traditional banking, where accounts can be frozen or transactions reversed at the institution's discretion.

Supply Mechanics: The fixed supply of Bitcoin contrasts sharply with the elastic supply of fiat currencies, where central banks can adjust monetary policy and influence inflation. Bitcoin's deflationary model is designed to preserve value over time.

Cross-Border Transactions: Bitcoin's digital nature enables seamless cross-border transactions without the need for currency exchange or the involvement of banks, often resulting in lower fees and faster settlement times than traditional international transfers.

In summary, Bitcoin introduces a new paradigm in the concept of money, offering a decentralized, secure, and digital alternative to traditional fiat currencies. Its unique properties and growing acceptance position it as a significant player in the future of finance.

The History of Bitcoin

Origins

The story of Bitcoin begins in 2008 when an individual or group operating under the pseudonym Satoshi Nakamoto published the Bitcoin whitepaper. This seminal document, titled "Bitcoin: A Peer-to-Peer Electronic Cash System," proposed a revolutionary new form of currency designed to work without a central authority. Instead, it would operate on a peer-to-peer network, solving the long-standing problem of double-spending in digital currencies through an innovative use of cryptographic proof instead of trust.

In January 2009, the Bitcoin network came to life with the mining of the genesis block, known as Block 0. This marked the birth of the Bitcoin blockchain and the creation of the first Bitcoins. Embedded within this block was a reference to a Times article, hinting at the motivation behind Bitcoin's creation: "The Times 03/Jan/2009 Chancellor on brink of second bailout for banks." This message underscored Bitcoin's aim to offer an alternative to the faltering traditional financial system, plagued by the 2008 financial crisis.

Early Days and Growth

The early days of Bitcoin were characterized by a tight-knit community of tech enthusiasts and libertarians, intrigued by the potential of a decentralized currency. The first-ever Bitcoin transaction occurred in January 2009 between Satoshi Nakamoto and computer scientist Hal Finney, demonstrating the network's capabilities.

As the community grew, so did the ecosystem around Bitcoin. The first Bitcoin exchange, BitcoinMarket.com, was established in 2010, providing a platform for trading Bitcoin for fiat currencies. This period also saw the development of the first Bitcoin wallet software, making it easier for non-technical users to store and manage their Bitcoins.

The true potential of Bitcoin as a medium of exchange was highlighted in May 2010 when programmer Laszlo Hanyecz made the first known purchase of a physical good using

Bitcoin, buying two pizzas for 10,000 Bitcoins, a transaction now celebrated annually as "Bitcoin Pizza Day."

Milestones

Bitcoin's journey is dotted with numerous significant milestones that have shaped its evolution. One of the most iconic moments occurred in 2010 with the aforementioned Bitcoin Pizza Day, illustrating Bitcoin's real-world value. Over the years, Bitcoin has achieved remarkable price milestones, breaking the $1,000 mark in 2013 and soaring past $20,000 in 2017, drawing widespread media attention and public interest.

Regulatory milestones have also been pivotal in Bitcoin's history. Various countries have grappled with how to regulate Bitcoin, with some embracing it and others imposing strict controls or outright bans. Notable regulatory events include the U.S. Senate's first hearing on Bitcoin in 2013, which acknowledged its legitimate uses, and Japan's recognition of Bitcoin as a legal payment method in 2017, which bolstered its legitimacy globally.

Challenges and Resilience

Despite its successes, Bitcoin has faced its share of challenges. Regulatory scrutiny has been a constant theme, with governments worldwide struggling to understand and manage the implications of a decentralized currency. Security issues have also been a concern, highlighted by high-profile hacks and scams, such as the Mt. Gox exchange collapse in 2014.

Bitcoin's price volatility has been another challenge, with dramatic swings that have tested the resolve of investors and users. Despite these hurdles, Bitcoin has shown remarkable resilience, bouncing back from setbacks and continuing to grow in both value and adoption. Its ability to withstand these challenges speaks to the strength of its underlying technology and the robust community that supports it.

This resilience, combined with continued innovation and growing acceptance, suggests that Bitcoin is not just a fleeting experiment but a transformative technology with the potential to reshape the financial landscape.

How Bitcoin Works

Blockchain Technology

At the heart of Bitcoin is blockchain technology, a decentralized and public ledger that records every transaction made within the network. Imagine the blockchain as a chain of digital "blocks," each containing a list of transactions. Once a block is filled with transactions, it is added to the chain in a linear, chronological order, creating a comprehensive and immutable record of all transactions ever made.

This decentralized nature of the blockchain means it is not stored in a central location but distributed across a vast network of computers, known as nodes. Each node has a copy of the entire blockchain, and any changes made to one copy are replicated across all copies. This ensures a high level of security and transparency, as altering any information on the blockchain would require an impossible amount of computing power to change every copy simultaneously.

The blockchain's design inherently protects against fraud and unauthorized alterations, using cryptographic hash functions to link each block to its predecessor. This creates an unbreakable chain, as altering a single block would invalidate all subsequent blocks, making tampering immediately evident.

Transactions and the Network

Bitcoin transactions begin with the creation of a digital wallet, which generates a pair of cryptographic keys: a public key, which acts as your Bitcoin address, and a private key, used to authorize transactions. When you initiate a Bitcoin transaction, you're essentially creating a digital message that specifies the amount of Bitcoin you wish to send and the recipient's address.

This transaction is then broadcast to the Bitcoin network, where it awaits confirmation. Network participants, known as miners, gather multiple transactions from the pool of unconfirmed transactions and compile them into a block. Miners then compete to validate the transactions within the block by solving a complex cryptographic puzzle, a process known as proof of work.

The first miner to solve the puzzle gets to add the new block to the blockchain, and the transactions within the block are considered confirmed. This process not only validates transactions but also ensures the network's security and integrity.

Mining and New Bitcoins

Mining is the process by which new Bitcoins are created and transactions are verified and added to the blockchain. Miners use powerful computers to solve complex mathematical problems that validate transactions and secure the network. The first miner to solve the problem gets to add a new block to the blockchain and is rewarded with newly minted Bitcoins (known as the block reward) and transaction fees.

The concept of a 'block' is fundamental to blockchain technology. Each block contains a list of transactions, and once a block is added to the blockchain, the transactions within are considered confirmed and irreversible. The block reward serves as an incentive for miners to contribute their computing power to the network, securing the blockchain and processing transactions.

The block reward is halved approximately every four years in an event known as "halving," which gradually reduces the rate at which new Bitcoins are created until the maximum supply of 21 million is reached. This controlled supply is one of Bitcoin's key features, designed to mimic the scarcity and value preservation of precious metals like gold.

Security and Privacy

The security of the Bitcoin network is underpinned by cryptographic principles, particularly the use of public and private keys. Your public key is derived from your private key and serves as your Bitcoin address, which you share with others to receive Bitcoin. The private key, which you must keep secret, is used to sign transactions and prove ownership of your Bitcoin.

This use of cryptography ensures that only the owner of the private key can authorize transactions, providing a high level of security. Moreover, all transactions are encrypted and recorded on the public blockchain, allowing anyone to verify transactions independently while keeping the identities of the parties involved anonymous.

Bitcoin maintains user privacy through the use of pseudonymous addresses. While the transaction history of each address is public, the real-world identity of the users behind the addresses is not inherently revealed. This system provides a balance between transparency, allowing the network to verify transactions, and privacy, protecting users' identities. However, it's worth noting that Bitcoin's privacy can be compromised if an individual's Bitcoin address is linked to their identity through other means, such as exchanges or transactions involving personal information.

Blockchain Technology

In the digital age, a groundbreaking innovation has emerged with the power to redefine the very foundations of our economic, social, and technological landscapes: blockchain technology. Imagine a world where transactions, agreements, and data are not just secure but transparent, immutable, and decentralized, free from the control of any central authority. This is the promise of blockchain, a promise that began with Bitcoin and has since captivated minds and sparked revolutions across industries worldwide.

At the heart of Bitcoin, blockchain serves as the bedrock, a public ledger that is both open and cryptographically secure, ensuring the integrity of every transaction without the need for traditional intermediaries like banks. Yet, the implications of blockchain extend far beyond Bitcoin. This technology is paving the way for a new era of digital innovation, offering a platform for smart contracts, decentralized applications, and an array of uses that span from supply chain management to digital identity verification.

In this chapter, we embark on a journey to unravel the complexities of blockchain technology. We'll explore its origins, delve into its core mechanics, and uncover how it functions as the engine behind Bitcoin. But our exploration won't stop there. We'll also venture into the myriad applications of blockchain, shedding light on its potential to transform industries, redefine trust, and create a future where transparency, security, and decentralization reign supreme. The revolution has just begun, and blockchain stands at its forefront, promising a world where digital transactions and data are safeguarded in an unprecedented fortress of cryptographic veracity.

Understanding the Blockchain

Foundations of Blockchain

At its core, blockchain is a revolutionary ledger technology, where "blocks" of data are linked and secured using cryptography, forming a continuous, unalterable chain. Unlike traditional ledgers maintained by a single entity, blockchain is decentralized; its distributed nature means the ledger is held and updated by multiple participants across a network, ensuring no single point of failure or control.

This decentralized approach is underpinned by cryptographic principles, ensuring the integrity and security of data recorded on the blockchain. Each transaction is encrypted and linked to the previous one, creating a secure and immutable record. The decentralized nature not only democratizes data management but also significantly enhances security, as tampering with data on one node would require simultaneous alterations across the majority of the network, a feat nearly impossible to achieve due to the cryptographic safeguards in place.

Transactions on a blockchain are grouped into blocks, each with a finite capacity. Once a block is filled with transactions, it is cryptographically sealed and added to the chain. This addition is permanent; the history of transactions becomes an unalterable ledger, providing a transparent and verifiable record of all transactions ever made.

Blockchain Structure

The structure of a blockchain is elegantly simple yet profoundly impactful. At its most basic level, a blockchain is a series of blocks, each containing a list of transactions. Every block is linked to the previous one through a cryptographic hash, a unique digital fingerprint that ensures the integrity of the block and its place in the chain.

Each block comprises several key elements: a block header, which includes the cryptographic hash of the previous block, thus linking them together; a timestamp, marking the time of block creation; and the transactions themselves, each securely encrypted. The first block in a chain, known as the genesis block, is unique in that it has no predecessor.

The true power of blockchain lies in its distributed ledger technology. Copies of the ledger are held across multiple nodes in the network, each node working to validate and record transactions. This redundancy ensures that even if one or more nodes are compromised, the overall integrity and continuity of the ledger remain intact.

Consensus Mechanisms

Consensus mechanisms are the heartbeats of blockchain technology, ensuring all participants in the network agree on the validity of transactions and the addition of new blocks to the chain. These mechanisms are critical for maintaining the integrity and trust of the blockchain, especially in decentralized networks where no central authority dictates the state of the ledger.

Proof of Work (PoW) and Proof of Stake (PoS) are two primary consensus mechanisms. PoW, used by Bitcoin, involves solving complex cryptographic puzzles to validate transactions and create new blocks, a process known as mining. This mechanism ensures security and decentralization but is often criticized for its high energy consumption.

On the other hand, PoS offers a more energy-efficient alternative, where the probability of validating transactions and creating new blocks is proportional to the amount of currency a participant holds. This not only reduces energy consumption but also encourages a more equitable distribution of power among stakeholders.

Security and Transparency

Blockchain's unique structure provides an unparalleled level of security and transparency. The use of cryptographic hashes in linking blocks ensures that once a block is added to the chain, altering its content retroactively becomes computationally infeasible. This immutability is a cornerstone of blockchain's security, deterring fraud and tampering.

Transparency is achieved through the public nature of the blockchain ledger. Every participant in the network can view the history of transactions, fostering a level of openness and trust not possible in traditional centralized systems. However, this transparency does not compromise privacy; while all transactions are visible, the parties involved can remain anonymous or pseudonymous, protected by cryptographic techniques.

Despite its strengths, blockchain is not without its challenges and misconceptions. Concerns over scalability, privacy, and regulatory compliance are often cited. However, ongoing innovations and adaptations in blockchain technology continue to address these issues, promising a future where the benefits of security and transparency are accessible to all.

The Role of Blockchain in Bitcoin

Blockchain as the Backbone of Bitcoin

Blockchain technology is the cornerstone upon which Bitcoin, the first and most well-known cryptocurrency, is built. This ingenious system provides a secure and decentralized framework for recording transactions, thereby enabling the existence of a digital currency free from central authority control. At its essence, the blockchain acts as a public ledger, an immutable record of all transactions ever made in the Bitcoin network, ensuring transparency and trust among its users.

The blockchain's decentralized nature means that no single entity owns or controls the Bitcoin network. Instead, it relies on a peer-to-peer network of nodes, each holding a copy of the blockchain, to validate and record transactions. This setup ensures that Bitcoin remains a democratic form of digital currency, resistant to censorship and immune to the control of any government or financial institution.

Each transaction on the Bitcoin network is broadcast to this network of nodes, which then uses complex algorithms to verify the transaction's validity. Once verified, transactions are grouped into blocks and added to the blockchain through a consensus mechanism known as Proof of Work. This process not only secures the network but also introduces new bitcoins into circulation as a reward for the computational work done by the miners, thus aligning the incentives of network participants with the security and integrity of the system.

Mining and Transaction Verification

Mining is the lifeblood of the Bitcoin ecosystem, a critical process that involves verifying transactions and adding them to the blockchain. Miners, using powerful computers, solve complex mathematical problems that validate groups of transactions, which are then compiled into a block. This block is linked to the previous one, forming a chain that securely records every transaction in the history of Bitcoin.

The mining process serves a dual purpose: it ensures the integrity and chronological order of the blockchain and introduces new bitcoins into the system as a reward for the miners' computational efforts. The reward, known as the block reward, is halved approximately every four years in an event known as "halving," ensuring that the total supply of bitcoins approaches but never exceeds 21 million.

Transaction verification is an integral part of mining. Each transaction must be checked for its validity, which includes ensuring that the digital signatures are correct and that the transaction does not attempt to spend bitcoins that have already been spent. This system of verification and consensus through mining is what makes Bitcoin secure and prevents double-spending, a significant concern for digital currencies.

Decentralization and Trust

Decentralization is a fundamental aspect of Bitcoin, setting it apart from traditional currencies and financial systems. By distributing the ledger across a wide network of computers, Bitcoin eliminates the need for a central authority, such as a bank or government, to validate transactions. This decentralization ensures that no single entity can control or manipulate the currency, thereby fostering a greater level of trust among its users.

In the Bitcoin network, trust is achieved not through intermediaries but through cryptography and consensus mechanisms. Users trust the system's integrity because the rules of Bitcoin are open, transparent, and enforced by the collective agreement of the network participants.

This trust is further reinforced by the fact that anyone can participate in the Bitcoin network, whether by transacting, running a node, or mining, contributing to the system's security and resilience.

Challenges and Limitations

Despite its revolutionary potential, blockchain technology, as applied in Bitcoin, faces several challenges and limitations. Scalability remains a significant concern, as the Bitcoin network can only process a limited number of transactions per second, leading to potential bottlenecks during times of high demand. Various solutions, such as the Lightning Network, have been proposed to address this issue, but they are still in the development or early adoption stages.

Energy consumption is another critical challenge facing Bitcoin mining. The Proof of Work consensus mechanism, while secure, requires a substantial amount of computational power, leading to high energy consumption. This has raised environmental concerns and calls for more sustainable alternatives, such as Proof of

Stake, which Ethereum and other cryptocurrencies are exploring.

Additionally, regulatory and legal challenges pose obstacles to the widespread adoption of Bitcoin. The decentralized and anonymous nature of Bitcoin makes it difficult for governments and regulatory bodies to oversee and control, leading to concerns about its use for illegal activities. As a result, Bitcoin and other cryptocurrencies face varying levels of scrutiny and regulation in different jurisdictions, affecting their acceptance and use.

Despite these challenges, the role of blockchain in Bitcoin represents a significant leap forward in the development of digital currencies and decentralized systems. Its ability to provide a secure, transparent, and decentralized ledger for financial transactions has not only given rise to the cryptocurrency movement but also inspired countless innovations in various sectors, highlighting the transformative potential of blockchain technology.

Implications and Uses of Blockchain

Beyond Bitcoin: Blockchain's Broader Applications

While Bitcoin introduced the world to blockchain, the technology's potential applications extend far beyond cryptocurrencies. In finance, blockchain is revolutionizing traditional practices by enabling faster, more secure, and transparent transactions. Smart contracts, automated agreements executed on the blockchain, are eliminating the need for intermediaries in financial services, from loans and insurance to asset management and international payments.

The supply chain industry is another significant beneficiary of blockchain. By providing a transparent and immutable record of transactions, blockchain technology allows for the tracking of goods from production to delivery, enhancing transparency, reducing fraud, and improving efficiency. This capability is particularly valuable in sectors where authenticity and origin verification are crucial, such as in the pharmaceutical and luxury goods industries.

Identity verification is another area where blockchain is making strides. By offering a secure and unforgeable way of managing digital identities, blockchain technology is paving the way for improved privacy and security in online transactions and services. This application is particularly relevant in the current era of frequent data breaches and identity theft, offering a more secure alternative to traditional methods of identity verification.

Smart Contracts and Decentralized Applications

Smart contracts are self-executing contracts with the terms of the agreement directly written into lines of code. These contracts automatically enforce and execute the terms of the agreement when predetermined conditions are met, without the need for intermediaries. This automation not only reduces the potential for disputes but also significantly lowers transaction costs and increases efficiency.

Decentralized applications (DApps) leverage smart contracts and blockchain technology to create applications that run on a peer-to-peer network, rather than on a single centralized server. This decentralization ensures that DApps are resistant to censorship, downtime, and control by a single authority, leading to a new wave of applications in fields as diverse as social media, gaming, and online marketplaces.

Impact on Industries

Blockchain technology is making a tangible impact across various industries, demonstrating its versatility and transformative potential. In the financial sector, blockchain is enabling cross-border payments to be conducted more quickly and with lower fees than traditional banking systems. The real estate industry is also benefiting from blockchain through tokenization, which allows property ownership to be divided into shares represented by digital tokens, making real estate investment more accessible and liquid.

Healthcare is another field where blockchain is making significant inroads. By providing a secure platform for storing and sharing patient data, blockchain technology is enhancing privacy, security, and interoperability in healthcare systems. Additionally, in the energy sector, blockchain is facilitating the creation of decentralized energy grids, allowing for more efficient distribution and trading of energy.

Future Prospects and Challenges

As blockchain technology continues to evolve, its future prospects are vast. The ongoing development of blockchain infrastructure and the increasing integration of artificial intelligence and the Internet of Things (IoT) are expected to unlock new capabilities and applications, from more sophisticated smart contracts to fully autonomous DApps.

However, the journey ahead is not without challenges. Scalability remains a significant hurdle, with many blockchain networks struggling to handle high volumes of transactions efficiently. Interoperability between different blockchain platforms is also an area that requires further development to enable seamless communication and transaction across various networks.

Regulatory uncertainty and legal challenges also pose significant obstacles to the widespread adoption of blockchain technology. As the technology continues to mature, regulatory frameworks will need to evolve to provide clear guidelines and support innovation while protecting consumers and ensuring stability in financial markets.

Despite these challenges, the potential of blockchain technology is undeniable. Its ability to provide secure, transparent, and decentralized solutions has already begun to transform industries, and as the technology matures, its impact is set to become even more profound. The future of blockchain is bright, promising a world where digital transactions and data are more secure, efficient, and equitable.

In Chapter 2, we embarked on a comprehensive journey through the intricacies of blockchain technology, starting with its foundational role as the backbone of Bitcoin. We explored how this innovative technology not only underpins the world's first digital currency but also offers a new paradigm for secure, transparent, and decentralized transactions. The process of mining and transaction verification was delved into, highlighting the meticulous mechanisms that maintain the integrity and trust of the Bitcoin network.

We then broadened our perspective to uncover the vast implications and applications of blockchain beyond the realm of cryptocurrencies. From revolutionizing financial transactions and supply chains to transforming identity verification processes, blockchain's versatility is unmistakable. The advent of smart contracts and decentralized applications (DApps) was discussed, showcasing how blockchain is redefining traditional agreements and services with unprecedented efficiency and security.

The impact of blockchain across various industries was also examined, revealing real-world examples of how this technology is driving innovation and solving long-standing challenges in sectors as diverse as healthcare, real estate, and energy. These case studies serve as a testament to blockchain's transformative potential and its ability to facilitate more transparent, efficient, and equitable systems.

Looking ahead, we contemplated the future prospects and challenges of blockchain technology. While the path forward is filled with immense potential, hurdles such as scalability, interoperability, and regulatory uncertainties remain. Addressing these challenges will be crucial for unlocking the full promise of blockchain and fostering its widespread adoption.

As we conclude this chapter, it's clear that blockchain technology is not just a fleeting trend but a revolutionary force with the power to reshape industries, redefine trust, and democratize access to information and resources. Its groundbreaking nature lies not only in its technical capabilities but also in its potential to empower individuals and communities around the globe.

This exploration is merely the beginning. As readers, you are encouraged to dive deeper into the world of blockchain, to question, learn, and engage with this technology. The future of blockchain is still being written, and you have the opportunity to be part of this exciting journey. Whether you're an innovator, investor, or simply a curious mind, the time is ripe to explore the endless possibilities that blockchain presents. Together, we can navigate this new digital frontier, contributing to a future where technology serves as a foundation for fairness, transparency, and inclusivity.

Buying and Storing Bitcoin

Embarking on the journey of purchasing Bitcoin is not just about acquiring a piece of digital currency; it's about participating in a financial revolution that is democratizing wealth and investment opportunities across the globe. Bitcoin, the pioneer of cryptocurrencies, embodies a shift towards a decentralized and transparent financial system, free from the constraints of traditional banking institutions. Understanding how to buy Bitcoin is the first step into this new world, where the power of finance is redistributed into the hands of the individual.

This section is designed to demystify the process of buying Bitcoin, breaking down perceived complexities into simple, actionable steps. Whether you're a seasoned investor or a curious newcomer, the path to owning Bitcoin is more straightforward than it appears. We'll guide you through the nuances of marketplaces, the setup of your first purchase, and the execution of a transaction with clarity and precision. Our aim is to equip you with the knowledge and confidence needed to make your foray into Bitcoin not just successful, but also empowering. As you turn the page, prepare to unlock the doors to a new financial frontier, where your journey is limited only by your curiosity and ambition.

In the ever-evolving landscape of digital currency, Bitcoin stands as a beacon of potential and innovation, drawing in a diverse audience eager to partake in its growth. To navigate this terrain, understanding the various marketplaces for purchasing Bitcoin is essential. Each platform presents its unique features, catering to different preferences and needs.

Cryptocurrency Exchanges

Cryptocurrency exchanges are the cornerstone of Bitcoin trading, offering a digital marketplace where individuals can exchange fiat currencies, like USD or EUR, for Bitcoin. These platforms stand out for their global accessibility, allowing users from around the world to engage in trading activities. With high liquidity, they facilitate smooth and rapid transactions, ensuring that buy or sell orders are executed promptly. Moreover, exchanges offer a wide array of trading pairs, not limited to fiat-to-Bitcoin but also encompassing various cryptocurrency pairs, enabling users to diversify their portfolio within the same platform.

Advantages:

Global Accessibility: Virtually anyone with internet access can participate, breaking down geographical barriers to entry.

High Liquidity: Large volumes of trading ensure that transactions can be completed quickly and at desired prices.

Diverse Trading Options: A wide range of trading pairs allows for greater flexibility in investment strategies.

Disadvantages:

Complexity for Beginners: The plethora of options and sophisticated trading interfaces might overwhelm new users.

Security Concerns: Despite advancements, exchanges remain targets for hackers, necessitating stringent security measures.

Regulatory Scrutiny: Being centralized entities, they are subject to government regulations, which can affect their operation and the privacy of users.

Peer-to-Peer (P2P) Networks

Peer-to-Peer networks offer a more personalized approach to buying Bitcoin, connecting buyers and sellers directly. This method emphasizes personal interaction, allowing for negotiation on price and terms of trade. P2P platforms often provide a rating system for users, fostering a sense of trust and community. This marketplace is ideal for those seeking competitive rates and more control over their transactions.

Advantages:

Direct Transactions: Eliminates the need for intermediaries, potentially reducing fees and increasing privacy.

Negotiation Flexibility: Prices and payment methods can be negotiated directly between parties, offering more control over the transaction.

Enhanced Privacy: Transactions can be less traceable compared to centralized exchanges, appealing to those valuing anonymity.

Disadvantages:

Risk of Fraud: Without a centralized authority, the risk of encountering fraudulent users increases.

Learning Curve: Understanding how to assess the reliability of trading partners and negotiate effectively can be daunting for newcomers.

Varied Liquidity: Depending on the platform and region, finding a suitable trade can sometimes be challenging.

Bitcoin ATMs

Bitcoin ATMs merge the digital world of cryptocurrency with the tangible, providing physical kiosks where individuals can purchase Bitcoin using cash or debit cards. Their straightforward interface resembles traditional ATMs, making them an approachable option for those new to Bitcoin. Positioned in various locations, they serve as a bridge for the unbanked population to access digital currency.

Advantages:

Ease of Use: The familiar ATM interface simplifies the purchasing process for beginners.

Immediate Acquisition: Transactions are completed on the spot, providing instant possession of Bitcoin.

Accessibility: Serves as a valuable resource for individuals without access to traditional banking services.

Disadvantages:

Higher Fees: Convenience comes at a cost, with ATMs often charging higher transaction fees.

Limited Availability: While growing, the distribution of Bitcoin ATMs is uneven, with higher concentrations in urban areas.

Purchase Limits: Many ATMs impose limits on the amount of Bitcoin that can be purchased, which may be restrictive for some users.

Navigating the diverse landscape of Bitcoin marketplaces requires understanding the unique attributes of each platform. Whether prioritizing ease of use, security, privacy, or accessibility, there's a marketplace tailored to every user's needs, marking the first step toward unlocking the potential of Bitcoin.

Setting up your first Bitcoin purchase is a pivotal moment in your journey into the world of cryptocurrency. This section will walk you through the essential steps, ensuring you approach this venture with confidence and security.

Setting Up a Purchase

Choosing an Exchange

The first step in buying Bitcoin is selecting a suitable exchange. Think of an exchange as your gateway to the world of cryptocurrency, where you'll conduct your transactions. When choosing an exchange, consider the following factors:

Security: Look for exchanges that have robust security measures in place, such as two-factor authentication, cold storage options for funds, and a track record of handling security breaches professionally.

Fees: Understand the fee structure of the exchange, including trading fees, withdrawal fees, and any other potential charges. Lower fees can significantly affect your investment over time.

User Interface: Especially important for beginners, the platform should be user-friendly and intuitive. Many exchanges offer demo accounts, so take advantage of these to get a feel for the platform.

Regulatory Compliance: Ensure the exchange complies with relevant regulations in your jurisdiction. This compliance is a good indicator of the platform's reliability and security.

Account Creation and Verification

Once you've chosen an exchange, the next steps involve setting up your account and going through the verification process:

Sign Up: This usually involves providing an email address and creating a password. Some exchanges might ask for more information at this stage.

Verification: Due to regulatory requirements, most reputable exchanges will require you to verify your identity. This process, often referred to as Know Your Customer (KYC), typically requires submitting identification documents such as a passport or driver's license.

Security Measures: Enhance the security of your account by enabling features like two-factor authentication (2FA), which adds an extra layer of security beyond just a password.

Linking Payment Methods

With your account set up, you'll need to link a payment method to deposit fiat currency (like USD, EUR) that you'll use to buy Bitcoin:

Bank Accounts: Direct bank transfers are commonly used for their low fees, but they can take longer to process compared to other methods.

Credit/Debit Cards: These offer instant purchases but often come with higher fees and lower purchase limits.

E-Wallets: Digital wallets can offer a balance between speed and fees, depending on the exchange and your location.

Consider the trade-offs between speed, convenience, and cost when choosing your payment method.

Understanding Fees

Before executing your first purchase, it's crucial to understand the fees involved:

Trading Fees: Most exchanges charge a fee per trade, which can be a flat fee or a percentage of the trade volume.

Withdrawal Fees: There may be fees for withdrawing Bitcoin to your personal wallet, which vary by exchange.

Hidden Costs: Be aware of any potential hidden costs, such as unfavourable exchange rates or fees for inactive accounts.

Understanding these fees will help you make more informed decisions and manage your investments more effectively.

By following these steps, you'll be well-prepared to make your first Bitcoin purchase. Remember, the world of cryptocurrency is dynamic and ever-evolving, so continuous learning and adaptation are key to navigating it successfully.

Executing a Bitcoin transaction is the crescendo of your initial foray into cryptocurrency. This process involves several critical steps, each contributing to the successful acquisition of Bitcoin. Understanding these steps not only ensures a smooth transaction but also equips you with the knowledge to navigate the crypto market effectively.

Executing a Bitcoin Transaction

Order Types

When purchasing Bitcoin, you'll encounter mainly two types of orders: market orders and limit orders.

Market Orders allow you to buy Bitcoin instantly at the current market price. This order type is best when you want to execute a transaction quickly, without waiting for a specific price. **Limit Orders** give you the ability to set a specific price at which you're willing to buy Bitcoin. The order will only execute when the market price matches your set price. This type is advantageous for those aiming to buy at a lower price than the current market rate.

Understanding these order types is crucial for strategizing your purchases based on your financial goals and market conditions.

Reading the Market

Before placing an order, it's essential to interpret basic market data:

Price Charts: These provide a visual representation of Bitcoin's price movements over time, helping you identify trends and patterns.

Order Books: An order book lists all buy and sell orders in the market, offering insights into market depth, potential support and resistance levels, and the overall market sentiment.

A grasp of these elements can significantly enhance your decision-making process, enabling you to place orders more judiciously.

Finalizing the Transaction

To execute a purchase:

Choose Your Order Type: Decide whether a market order or a limit order best suits your current needs.

Enter Order Details: Specify the amount of Bitcoin you want to buy and, if placing a limit order, the price you're willing to pay.

Review and Confirm: Double-check the order details, including the total cost and associated fees, before confirming the transaction.

Monitor the Order: For market orders, the transaction should complete almost instantly. Limit orders may take longer, depending on market movements.

It's important to note that transaction times can vary based on network congestion and the exchange's processing speed.

Post-Purchase Steps

After purchasing Bitcoin, consider transferring it to a personal wallet for enhanced security. Keeping your Bitcoin in an exchange wallet exposes you to risks such as hacking or exchange insolvency. A personal wallet, especially a hardware wallet, offers you control over your private keys, significantly reducing the risk of loss.

This step marks the conclusion of your initial Bitcoin purchase but also sets the stage for deeper engagement with cryptocurrency, from secure storage solutions to potentially diversifying your crypto portfolio. Remember, every step forward in this dynamic domain is a leap towards mastering the art of digital finance.

Wallet Overview

The journey into the world of Bitcoin necessitates a fundamental tool: the Bitcoin wallet. Unlike a traditional wallet, which holds physical currency, a Bitcoin wallet is a digital entity that stores the cryptographic keys required to access and manage your Bitcoin. These keys, one public and one private, are the core of your interactions with the Bitcoin network, enabling transactions and ensuring security.

The choice of wallet is pivotal, as it directly influences the safety, accessibility, and management of your Bitcoin. With a plethora of options available, understanding the essence and functionality of Bitcoin wallets is essential. A well-chosen wallet not only secures your assets against unauthorized access but also provides a user-friendly interface for managing your investments. It's the bridge between the user and the vast, intricate world of cryptocurrency, making its selection a crucial decision in your Bitcoin journey.

Types of Wallets

Bitcoin wallets come in various forms, each with unique features catering to different needs and preferences.

Software Wallets:

Desktop Wallets: Installed on a personal computer, they offer full control over your assets and keys. Ideal for users seeking a balance between security and convenience.

Mobile Wallets: Apps for smartphones, perfect for everyday transactions and those requiring Bitcoin on the go. They combine convenience with reasonable security.

Web Wallets: Accessible through web browsers, they offer flexibility and ease of use but rely on third-party providers, posing additional security considerations.

Hardware Wallets: Physical devices designed to securely store private keys offline. They are the gold standard for security, ideal for storing large amounts of Bitcoin and for users prioritizing security over convenience.

Each type of wallet has its security features, from basic password protection to advanced encryption and cold storage capabilities. The usability varies, with some catering to tech-savvy users desiring extensive features, while others focus on simplicity for those new to Bitcoin.

Factors to Consider

Selecting the right Bitcoin wallet involves considering several critical factors:

Security: The foremost consideration, encompassing features like encryption, two-factor authentication, and the ability to control private keys.

Control: The degree of control you have over your keys and Bitcoin. Wallets allowing full control are preferable for security-conscious users.

Backup and Restoration: Features enabling easy backup and recovery of your wallet, essential for safeguarding against hardware failure or loss.

Multi-signature Support: An advanced security feature requiring multiple approvals for a transaction, enhancing protection against unauthorized access.

User Interface: The wallet's usability, including its interface design and ease of navigating through features, is crucial for a smooth user experience.

Customer Support: The availability and quality of support provided by the wallet service, significant for resolving issues and providing guidance.

Weighing these factors will guide you in choosing a wallet that aligns with your security needs, technical proficiency, and Bitcoin management preferences.

Recommendations and Examples

For beginners, simplicity and ease of use are paramount. Mobile wallets like *Mycelium* or web wallets such as *Blockchain.info* offer user-friendly interfaces and basic features suitable for daily transactions and small amounts of Bitcoin.

Intermediate users, balancing convenience with enhanced security, might prefer *Electrum* (a desktop wallet) known for its robust security features while still being reasonably straightforward to use.

Advanced users, or those holding significant amounts of Bitcoin, should consider hardware wallets like *Trezor* or *Ledger Nano S.* These devices provide the highest security level by keeping private keys offline and are ideal for long-term storage.

In each recommendation, real-world scenarios demonstrate the wallet's application, from daily spending to securing life-changing amounts of Bitcoin, painting a comprehensive picture of wallet setups across the user spectrum.

This section aims to navigate the diverse landscape of Bitcoin wallets, providing clarity and direction in selecting the most suitable wallet for your journey in the world of Bitcoin.

The Importance of Security

In the digital realm of Bitcoin, security is not just a precaution; it's a necessity. The decentralized nature of Bitcoin empowers users with unprecedented control over their assets, but this freedom comes with the responsibility of safeguarding them. Unlike traditional banking systems, where a forgotten password or a stolen card can be remedied with a phone call, Bitcoin operates on the principle of irreversibility. Transactions, once made, cannot be undone, and lost access to a wallet is a loss of the assets within it.

The risks of inadequate security measures are manifold, ranging from the all-too-common tales of forgotten private keys rendering fortunes inaccessible, to the more sinister scenarios of hacking and phishing attacks leading to direct theft. The digital world is rife with opportunistic entities poised to exploit any vulnerability. Therefore, securing your Bitcoin transcends mere precaution; it's the very foundation upon which the safe use of cryptocurrency is built.

Basic Security Measures

The first line of defence in securing your Bitcoin involves basic but crucial practices:

Strong, Unique Passwords: Every point of access, from your wallet to exchange accounts, should be protected by a strong, complex password, distinct from those used on any other platform. Tools like password managers can help manage these effectively.

Two-Factor Authentication (2FA): Elevate your security by enabling 2FA on all cryptocurrency-related accounts. This adds a layer of security beyond the password, typically requiring a code from a mobile device that only you possess.

Phishing Scams Awareness: Stay vigilant about phishing attempts, which often come in the form of emails or messages mimicking legitimate services to steal login information. Always verify the authenticity of communication and never disclose your private keys or passwords.

Implementing these basic measures can significantly fortify your defences against the most common security breaches.

Advanced Security Techniques

For those looking to bolster their Bitcoin security further, advanced techniques offer enhanced protection:

Multi-Signature Setups: Multi-signature arrangements require more than one private key to authorize a transaction, adding an extra layer of security by distributing the risk. This setup is particularly useful for organizations or partnerships.

Hardware Wallets: Storing your private keys on a hardware wallet keeps them offline, isolated from internet-based threats. These devices only connect to sign transactions, keeping your keys secure from online vulnerabilities.

Secure Backup Solutions: Regularly back up your wallet, storing the backup in a secure location separate from your primary residence. Consider using encrypted drives or even safe deposit boxes for critical backups.

Legacy and Inheritance Planning: Cryptocurrency assets can be lost forever if not properly planned for in estate planning. Solutions include ensuring trusted family members know how to access your assets in your absence or using specialized services that support digital inheritance.

These advanced measures require a higher level of engagement and understanding but are invaluable for those holding significant assets in Bitcoin.

Staying Updated

The final pillar of Bitcoin security is the commitment to continuous learning and adaptation:

Software Updates: Regularly update your wallet software and any associated applications. Updates often contain security enhancements and patches for known vulnerabilities.

Community Engagement: The Bitcoin community is a vibrant source of information, offering insights into emerging threats and best practices. Engage with forums, attend webinars, and participate in discussions to stay informed.

Emergency Preparedness: Have a clear plan in case of a security breach, including steps to isolate affected systems, change passwords, and recover assets if possible. Knowing how to react swiftly can mitigate potential losses.

In the ever-evolving landscape of cryptocurrency, staying informed and proactive about security is not just advantageous; it's essential. By embracing both foundational practices and advanced strategies, you can navigate the world of Bitcoin with confidence, safeguarding your digital treasures against the myriad of threats that lurk within the digital frontier.

Bitcoin Mining

What is Bitcoin Mining?

In the Bitcoin world, Bitcoin mining emerges as a cornerstone, underpinning the very fabric of the Bitcoin ecosystem. This process is not just about the creation of new bitcoins but also about maintaining and securing a decentralized ledger, known as the blockchain. At its core, Bitcoin mining is akin to a competitive lottery that makes fraudulent activities prohibitively expensive and thus secures the network against malicious actors.

The journey of Bitcoin mining is a tale of relentless evolution, a testament to the human quest for efficiency and innovation. In the nascent days of Bitcoin, enthusiasts could mine using simple CPU (Central Processing Unit) systems, the very heart of personal computers. This era was marked by accessibility, where anyone with a computer could contribute to the network. However, as the network grew and the mining difficulty increased, the stage was set for a transformative shift. GPUs (Graphics Processing Units), with their superior processing power, soon became the mining standard, heralding a new era of heightened efficiency and competition. Yet, the relentless march of progress did not halt there; FPGAs (Field-Programmable Gate Arrays) entered the scene, offering further optimizations before the advent of ASICs (Application-Specific Integrated Circuits). ASICs, designed exclusively for Bitcoin mining, represent the pinnacle of mining technology, offering unmatched efficiency and processing power.

At the heart of Bitcoin mining lies the Proof of Work (PoW) algorithm, a brilliantly simple yet profoundly effective mechanism. PoW requires miners to solve complex cryptographic puzzles, a process that demands considerable computational power and energy. The solution to these puzzles is arduous to find but easy to verify, ensuring that any attempts to tamper with the network are economically unfeasible and thus securing Bitcoin's ledger against alterations. This ingenious system not only guards against double-spending and ensures the integrity of the transaction history but also facilitates the decentralized consensus essential to Bitcoin's operation.

The allure of Bitcoin mining is not solely in the pursuit of securing the network but also in the tangible rewards it offers. Miners are rewarded with newly minted bitcoins, a process elegantly embedded in the mining activity, which simultaneously releases new coins into circulation and incentivizes miners to contribute their computational power. This block reward, halved approximately every four years in an event known as "halving," ensures a predictable and diminishing issuance of new bitcoins, mimicking the extraction of precious metals and underscoring Bitcoin's moniker as 'digital gold.' In addition to the block reward, miners also collect transaction fees, providing an additional incentive to process transactions and maintain the network's fluidity, especially as the block reward diminishes over time.

Bitcoin mining, therefore, stands as a testament to the symbiotic relationship between innovation and incentive, a dance of technology and economics that secures the Bitcoin network while fostering a decentralized, competitive mining industry. As we stand on the cusp of new advancements and challenges, Bitcoin mining continues to evolve, reflecting the dynamic and ever-changing landscape of cryptocurrency.

How Bitcoin Mining Works

At the intersection of finance and technology, Bitcoin mining emerges as a critical yet often misunderstood cog in the cryptocurrency wheel. In essence, mining is the process through which new bitcoins are created and transactions are added to Bitcoin's public ledger, the blockchain. It's a complex blend of cryptography, mathematics, and computer science, but at its core, Bitcoin mining is about solving puzzles to keep the network secure and functional.

Imagine a vast, decentralized network of computers, all working together yet independently, competing to solve a cryptographic puzzle. This puzzle involves taking transaction data, which is essentially a list of recent Bitcoin transactions waiting to be confirmed, and transforming it into a compact, unique 'summary' known as a hash. This hash must meet certain criteria set by the network—specifically, it must be less than a particular value. The process is akin to guessing a combination to a lock, where the 'lock' is the puzzle set by the network, and the 'combination' is the correct hash.

The first miner to find a hash that meets the network's criteria 'wins' the round, adding a new 'block' of transactions to the blockchain. This victorious miner is then rewarded with newly minted bitcoins and transaction fees. This entire process is what secures the blockchain, ensuring its integrity and chronological order through cryptographic means.

Delving deeper into the technicalities, the puzzles that miners solve are based on a cryptographic function called SHA-256. The difficulty of these puzzles adjusts automatically, ensuring that a new block is added to the blockchain approximately every ten minutes, regardless of the total computational power of the network. This self-adjusting mechanism is crucial for maintaining the blockchain's consistent and predictable growth.

As the complexity and competitive nature of mining have escalated, individual miners have found it increasingly difficult to compete. This challenge gave rise to mining pools—groups of miners who combine their computational resources to increase their chances of solving the puzzle and winning the reward. When a pool succeeds, the reward is distributed among its members, proportional to each miner's contribution of computational power.

The hardware required for Bitcoin mining has also evolved dramatically. Early miners used standard CPUs found in home computers, but as the difficulty increased, more powerful GPUs became the norm. Today, specialized equipment known as ASICs (Application-Specific Integrated Circuits) dominates the mining landscape. These devices are designed solely for Bitcoin mining, offering unparalleled efficiency but also representing significant investment and operational costs, including purchase price, maintenance, and electricity consumption.

This brings us to the significant environmental footprint of Bitcoin mining. The process is energy-intensive, primarily due to the computational power required to solve the cryptographic puzzles. The environmental impact has sparked debate and led to a push for more sustainable practices within the industry. Recent trends show a growing shift towards greener alternatives, such as using renewable energy sources like solar, wind, or hydroelectric power to run mining operations. Some mining operations are also exploring ways to utilize the excess heat generated by mining equipment, turning a byproduct into an asset for heating and other purposes.

In summary, Bitcoin mining is a complex process that lies at the heart of the Bitcoin ecosystem. It involves solving cryptographic puzzles to secure the network and process transactions, all while being rewarded with new bitcoins. The evolution from CPU to ASIC mining reflects the increasing complexity and competition within the space. Despite its environmental challenges, the mining community is gradually moving towards more sustainable practices, ensuring that Bitcoin mining remains a cornerstone of the cryptocurrency world while adapting to the pressing needs of our planet.

Should You Mine Bitcoin?

Venturing into the realm of Bitcoin mining is often driven by a blend of allure and altruism. On one hand, there's the enticing prospect of profit, the digital equivalent of finding a gold nugget in a stream. On the other, there's a deeper, more communal motive: supporting the decentralized network that Bitcoin embodies, contributing to the security and efficacy of this groundbreaking financial system.

The financial journey of Bitcoin mining begins with the initial investment. The days when a desktop computer could mine Bitcoin are long behind us, replaced by the need for specialized hardware, known as ASIC (Application-Specific Integrated Circuit) miners. The upfront cost of these machines can be substantial, often running into thousands of dollars for equipment that is at the cutting edge of efficiency. Beyond the hardware, there are ongoing expenses to consider: electricity costs are the most significant, given the energy-intensive nature of mining. Cooling systems to prevent overheating and maintenance to keep the hardware in prime condition also contribute to the operational costs.

The potential returns from mining are a complex equation, influenced by factors such as the current price of Bitcoin, the total network mining power, and the electricity cost at the miner's location. For instance, when Bitcoin's price soars, the rewards from mining can become particularly lucrative. However, these rewards are halved approximately every four years in an event known as the "halving," which can significantly impact profitability. Real-world examples abound of miners who've reaped substantial rewards during bull markets, only to struggle to cover their costs when the market turns bearish.

The volatile nature of Bitcoin's price adds a layer of risk to mining. The value of Bitcoin can swing wildly, affecting the potential rewards from mining. This volatility, coupled with the halving of block rewards, can turn mining from a profitable venture into a challenging one almost overnight. Regulatory concerns also loom large; different jurisdictions have varied stances on cryptocurrency, and policies can shift, potentially impacting the legality or cost-effectiveness of mining operations.

Moreover, the competitive landscape of mining has never been more fierce. As more miners join the network, the difficulty of mining increases, which can reduce the chances of earning rewards for individual miners or smaller pools. This competition necessitates continual investment in the latest hardware to remain viable, a cycle that can strain financial resources.

For those contemplating the mining voyage, it's crucial to weigh these considerations carefully. Mining can be a rewarding endeavor, both financially and in the sense of contributing to the Bitcoin network. However, it demands a significant commitment of time, resources, and energy. For individuals for whom direct mining may not be feasible, there are alternative pathways to involvement in the Bitcoin ecosystem. Investing directly in Bitcoin, participating in mining pools, or contributing to Bitcoin's development and spread are ways to engage without the hefty investment in mining infrastructure.

In conclusion, Bitcoin mining is a multifaceted venture, rich with potential but fraught with challenges. It requires a careful balance of technical acumen, financial resources, and a keen eye on the ever-shifting landscape of cryptocurrency. For those drawn to the pioneering spirit of Bitcoin, mining offers a unique way to engage with this digital revolution. Yet, for others, alternative paths to involvement may align more closely with their circumstances and goals, offering a way to be part of Bitcoin's journey without the complexities of mining.

Using Bitcoin

How to Use Bitcoin for Transactions

Introduction to Bitcoin Transactions

Bitcoin transactions stand as a paradigm of innovation, offering a decentralized and secure way to exchange value over the internet. Unlike traditional transactions that rely on intermediary financial institutions, Bitcoin operates on a peer-to-peer network, ensuring that each transaction is directly between users. This is made possible through the use of blockchain technology, a digital ledger that records all transactions chronologically and publicly. Each Bitcoin transaction is secured by cryptographic algorithms, ensuring integrity and preventing unauthorized alterations. This section will delve into the essence of Bitcoin transactions, shedding light on their revolutionary nature and the underlying technology that ensures security and decentralization.

Setting Up a Bitcoin Wallet

Venturing into the Bitcoin ecosystem, the foundational step is establishing a Bitcoin wallet, a pivotal component for engaging with this digital currency. This comprehensive guide illuminates the varied spectrum of Bitcoin wallets, including hardware, software, mobile, and paper options, each with distinct attributes and security considerations.

Hardware Wallets: The Fort Knox of Bitcoin Security
Hardware wallets are the epitome of security in the Bitcoin wallet sphere. These physical devices, resembling USB drives, securely store your private keys offline, safeguarding them from online vulnerabilities such as hacking and phishing. Renowned for their impenetrable nature, hardware wallets like *Ledger Nano S* and *Trezor* offer peace of mind, especially for substantial Bitcoin holdings. While they excel in security, their cost and the slight inconvenience of needing physical access for transactions are considerations for potential users.

Software Wallets: The Convenient Custodians

Software wallets, accessible as desktop or web applications, strike a balance between convenience and security. They store your private keys on a computer or online, facilitating easy access for daily transactions. Popular choices like *Electrum* and *Exodus* enchant users with their user-friendly interfaces and additional features such as in-wallet exchanges. However, their internet connectivity makes them more susceptible to cyber threats, necessitating robust cybersecurity measures, including regular software updates and comprehensive malware protection.

Mobile Wallets: Bitcoin at Your Fingertips

In the era of smartphones, mobile wallets offer unparalleled convenience, allowing users to execute transactions with a simple tap. Apps like *Mycelium* and *BRD* transform your mobile device into a portable Bitcoin hub, ideal for on-the-go payments and transfers. The integration of QR code scanning simplifies transactions, enhancing usability. Nevertheless, the convenience of mobile wallets is counterbalanced by security risks, particularly if the device is lost or compromised. Adopting security practices such as enabling multi-factor authentication and maintaining a backup of your wallet can mitigate these risks.

Paper Wallets: The Analog Anchors

Paper wallets, though less prevalent in the digital age, offer a unique form of Bitcoin storage. By printing your private and public keys on a piece of paper, you create a physical record of your Bitcoin holdings, immune to cyber-attacks. Services like *Bitcoin Paper Wallet* assist users in generating secure paper wallets. The main allure of paper wallets is their simplicity and detachment from digital threats. However, they are vulnerable to physical damage and loss, necessitating careful storage, perhaps in a safe or a secure location.

Choosing Your Bitcoin Wallet: Balancing Act Between Security and Convenience

Selecting the appropriate Bitcoin wallet hinges on your specific needs and preferences. For those prioritizing security over convenience, hardware wallets are the gold standard. Users seeking a blend of accessibility and security might lean towards software or mobile wallets, with a keen eye on cybersecurity practices. For transactions that mimic the tangibility of traditional currency, paper wallets provide an offline alternative.

In conclusion, embarking on the Bitcoin journey with the right wallet sets the stage for a secure and efficient experience. By carefully considering the unique features and security levels of each wallet type, you can select a solution that aligns with your transaction habits and security expectations, ensuring a seamless integration into the world of Bitcoin.

Initiating a Transaction

Initiating a Bitcoin transaction is a process that embodies the innovative essence of blockchain technology, allowing for the swift and efficient transfer of value worldwide. This journey from intention to execution is facilitated by a series of steps designed to ensure security, privacy, and efficiency. In this exploration, we'll unravel the complexities of initiating a Bitcoin transaction, from the creation of a unique address to the pivotal role of QR codes and the nuanced world of transaction fees.

Generating a Unique Address: The First Step
The inception of a Bitcoin transaction begins with the generation of a unique address. This alphanumeric string serves as the destination for the Bitcoin you wish to send. Comparable to an email address in the digital communication realm, this Bitcoin address ensures that the cryptocurrency reaches the intended recipient. Wallet software automates this process, generating a new address for each transaction to enhance privacy and security.

Leveraging QR Codes: Simplifying Transactions
In the pursuit of simplification and user convenience, QR codes have become a staple in Bitcoin transactions. These two-dimensional barcodes store information about the recipient's address and, optionally, the amount to be sent. Scanning a QR code with a mobile wallet app eliminates the need for manual address entry, minimizing the risk of errors and streamlining the

transaction process. This integration of QR codes into Bitcoin transactions exemplifies the synergy between traditional practices and modern technology, enhancing the user experience.

Understanding Transaction Fees: The Engine of Confirmation

Transaction fees are an integral component of the Bitcoin ecosystem, serving as the incentive for miners to process and confirm transactions. These fees are not fixed; instead, they fluctuate based on network congestion and the data size of the transaction. Users have the flexibility to set their fee, with higher fees typically resulting in faster confirmation times. It's a delicate balance between cost and urgency, as users must weigh the importance of speed against the potential expense. Wallets often provide a recommended fee based on current network conditions, guiding users towards an optimal choice.

The Transaction Process: From Initiation to Confirmation

Initiating a Bitcoin transaction involves entering the recipient's address, specifying the amount to send, and setting the transaction fee. Once this information is confirmed, the transaction is broadcasted to the Bitcoin network, awaiting validation by miners. These network participants use powerful computers to solve cryptographic puzzles, a process that secures the network and adds transactions to the blockchain. Upon successfully mining a block that includes your transaction, it achieves its first confirmation, with subsequent confirmations increasing security.

Ensuring a Seamless Experience

For a frictionless Bitcoin transaction experience, understanding the nuances of address generation, QR codes, and transaction fees is paramount. These components work in concert to provide a secure, efficient, and user-friendly process. By mastering these elements, users can confidently navigate the Bitcoin landscape, harnessing the full potential of this digital currency for global transactions.

Transaction Confirmation

The moment a Bitcoin transaction is broadcast to the network marks the beginning of its journey through the complex yet fascinating world of blockchain validation. This pivotal phase is not just a mere procedural step but the very backbone of Bitcoin's renowned security and reliability. Herein, we will dissect the intricacies of transaction confirmation, shedding light on the critical role played by miners and the profound significance of block confirmations.

The Miner's Quest: Guardians of the Blockchain

At the heart of the confirmation process are the miners, a network of participants armed with powerful computational resources. These digital prospectors engage in a relentless quest to solve cryptographic puzzles, a task that demands an immense computational effort. This endeavor is not merely for the pursuit of new bitcoins but serves a grander purpose in securing the Bitcoin network. Each puzzle solved represents a block of transactions that the miner proposes to add to the blockchain, effectively confirming these transactions.

Cryptographic Puzzles: The Gateway to Confirmation

The cryptographic puzzles that miners solve are ingeniously designed to maintain the integrity and pace of the blockchain. These puzzles require a specific output that can only be achieved by altering a nonce, a variable in the block header. The process, known as "Proof of Work," ensures that altering any part of the blockchain would require re-mining all subsequent blocks, a feat that would demand an unrealistic amount of computational power, thus safeguarding the network against tampering and double-spending.

The Race for Confirmation: A Competitive Process

Miners worldwide compete to solve these puzzles, with the first to succeed earning the right to add their proposed block to the blockchain. This addition, confirmed by other network participants, awards the successful miner with new bitcoins—a process known as the block reward—and transaction fees from the transactions included in the block. The competitive nature of mining ensures a decentralized and secure network, with multiple miners validating each transaction and maintaining the blockchain's integrity.

Block Confirmations: The Seal of Security
Upon the inclusion of a transaction in a newly mined block, it receives its first confirmation. However, the security of a transaction grows with each subsequent block added to the chain, burying the transaction deeper within the blockchain. A general rule of thumb suggests that six confirmations—approximately one hour's worth of mining—provide a high degree of security, making a transaction virtually irreversible.

The Significance of Confirmations

The confirmation process is the linchpin in the trust mechanism of Bitcoin transactions. It ensures that once a transaction is embedded in the blockchain, it becomes an immutable part of the ledger, protected against reversal or alteration. This robust security model fosters trust among participants, allowing for the secure, decentralized exchange of value that Bitcoin promises.

In sum, the journey from transaction broadcast to confirmation is a testament to the ingenuity of blockchain technology. It showcases a symphony of computational effort, competitive collaboration, and cryptographic security, ensuring that every Bitcoin transaction is secure, reliable, and, ultimately, immutable.

Safety and Security Tips

In the digital terrain of Bitcoin, where the stakes are as high as the potential rewards, security is not just a practice but a cornerstone of successful navigation. As you engage with this revolutionary currency, the sanctity of your digital assets hinges on a proactive and cautious approach to security. Herein, we lay down a tapestry of essential safety measures designed to shield your transactions and preserve your peace of mind.

Double-Check Addresses: Precision is Key

Before executing any transaction, take a moment to verify the recipient's address meticulously. A single digit or letter amiss can direct your Bitcoin into the abyss of the digital ether, an error often beyond rectification. Treat this step with the gravity it deserves, ensuring that your hard-earned assets reach their intended destination.

Secure Your Internet Connection: A Digital Moat

The allure of public Wi-Fi's convenience is undeniable, yet it's a siren call that often leads to perilous shores. When transacting in Bitcoin, ensure the sanctity of your internet connection; a secure, private network is your digital moat against the siege of hackers and interceptors.

Embrace a Culture of Caution: Your Digital Armor

In the vast expanse of the internet, your vigilance is your strongest ally. Be skeptical of unsolicited advice, double-check sources, and steer clear of dubious websites and links. In the realm of Bitcoin, where transactions are irreversible, caution is not just a virtue but a necessity.

Armed with these strategies, you stand ready to engage with the Bitcoin ecosystem, not as a mere participant but as a savvy steward of your digital treasures. Let these practices be the bedrock upon which you build your Bitcoin journey, ensuring that your venture into this digital frontier is both fruitful and secure.

Bitcoin in E-Commerce

Integrating Bitcoin Payments

In the evolving landscape of digital commerce, Bitcoin emerges as a transformative force, offering a novel avenue for transactional exchanges. The integration of Bitcoin into e-commerce platforms heralds a new era of financial interaction, characterized by decentralization, enhanced security, and borderless transactions. This section delves into the advantages of adopting Bitcoin as a payment method and provides a step-by-step guide for online stores to seamlessly incorporate Bitcoin payments, emphasizing the role of payment gateways and merchant services in this integration.

The process begins with selecting a reputable Bitcoin payment processor, which acts as a bridge between the merchant and the blockchain network. These processors offer tools and services to accept Bitcoin payments, convert them into local currencies, and deposit the funds into the merchant's account, mitigating the risks associated with price volatility. The integration typically involves adding a Bitcoin payment option at checkout, often facilitated by plugins or APIs provided by the payment processor, ensuring a smooth user experience for both the merchant and the customer.

Benefits for Merchants and Customers

Adopting Bitcoin as a payment method in e-commerce settings unlocks a plethora of benefits for both merchants and customers, fundamentally altering the dynamics of online transactions. For merchants, the allure of lower transaction fees compared to traditional payment methods is a significant draw, potentially boosting profitability. Furthermore, Bitcoin's global reach opens up international markets, allowing merchants to transact with customers across borders without the complexities and costs associated with currency conversion and cross-border fees.

Customers, on the other hand, enjoy the enhanced privacy and security afforded by Bitcoin transactions, which do not require the disclosure of sensitive personal information, thereby reducing the risk of identity theft. Additionally, the speed of Bitcoin transactions can surpass that of conventional bank transfers, particularly for international transactions, enhancing the customer experience.

However, the journey is not devoid of challenges, with price volatility being a notable concern. Fluctuations in Bitcoin's value can introduce complexities in pricing and profitability for merchants. Strategies such as instant conversion to fiat currency through payment processors and transparent communication with customers about pricing can mitigate these challenges.

Real-World Examples

The theoretical advantages of Bitcoin in e-commerce are brought to life through real-world applications, where businesses of varying scales have successfully integrated Bitcoin payments. This section showcases case studies of such businesses, highlighting the practicalities of implementation, the challenges encountered, and the solutions devised to overcome them. These narratives serve as a source of inspiration and a blueprint for other businesses considering a foray into Bitcoin payments.

From small online boutiques to large multinational corporations, the adoption of Bitcoin payments transcends industry boundaries, demonstrating the versatility and appeal of Bitcoin in the commercial domain. These examples not only underscore the tangible benefits realized by these pioneering entities but also shed light on the evolving consumer perception and acceptance of Bitcoin as a legitimate payment method.

Future Trends

As we gaze into the horizon of Bitcoin in e-commerce, the confluence of technological advancements and increasing adoption rates paints a promising picture of growth and innovation. This section explores speculative future developments, including the integration of Lightning Network to facilitate micropayments, the advent of smart contracts for automated and escrow transactions, and the potential for Bitcoin to become a staple in the arsenal of payment methods offered by e-commerce platforms.

The democratization of access to global markets, the emergence of new business models predicated on the unique attributes of Bitcoin, and the continuous improvement in user experience and security protocols are among the anticipated trends. As regulatory landscapes evolve and societal familiarity with cryptocurrency grows, we may witness a paradigm shift in how transactions are conducted in the digital marketplace, with Bitcoin playing a central role in this transformation.

In sum, the intersection of Bitcoin and e-commerce represents a frontier of opportunity, challenging conventional transactional paradigms and paving the way for a more inclusive, efficient, and secure commercial ecosystem.

Sending and Receiving Bitcoin

Basics of Sending Bitcoin

The act of sending Bitcoin is underpinned by a fascinating array of technical mechanisms, which ensure the integrity and security of transactions within the blockchain network. Central to this process are the concepts of transaction inputs, outputs, and the Unspent Transaction Outputs (UTXO) model, which collectively orchestrate the movement of Bitcoin between parties.

When a Bitcoin transaction is initiated, it essentially comprises one or more inputs, which are references to previous transactions indicating the source of the funds. Each input is like a digital fingerprint, unique and specific, ensuring that the same Bitcoin cannot be spent twice. The transaction then specifies its outputs, which detail the recipient addresses and the amount of Bitcoin being sent to each. This delineation of inputs and outputs facilitates the flow of value and information across the network.

The UTXO model plays a pivotal role in tracking Bitcoin ownership. UTXOs are essentially the Bitcoin amounts that have been received but not yet spent by an address. Each transaction checks these UTXOs to verify that the sender has sufficient funds. Once a transaction is confirmed, the used UTXOs become 'spent,' and new UTXOs are created for the recipients, ready to be used in future transactions. This continuous cycle of spending and receiving UTXOs is what dynamically maintains the state of Bitcoin ownership on the blockchain.

Receiving Bitcoin

Receiving Bitcoin is a straightforward process that entails having a Bitcoin address and sharing it with the party intending to send Bitcoin. A Bitcoin address is derived from the public key of a cryptographic key pair and serves as the destination for Bitcoin transactions. Generating a new address for each incoming transaction is a recommended practice for enhancing privacy, as it prevents transaction linkability which can compromise anonymity.

When sharing a Bitcoin address, it's common to use a QR code for ease and accuracy, reducing the risk of errors in address transcription. Once the sender initiates the transaction to the provided address and it's confirmed on the blockchain, the recipient will see the amount reflected in their wallet balance, underpinned by the creation of new UTXOs associated with the recipient's address.

Privacy considerations are paramount when receiving Bitcoin. The transparent nature of the blockchain means that transactions are publicly visible, so maintaining financial privacy requires careful management of addresses and transaction linkages. Using a new address for each transaction and employing privacy-enhancing tools or services can help mitigate these concerns.

Common Pitfalls

Navigating the Bitcoin network comes with its challenges, and being aware of common pitfalls can greatly enhance the security and efficiency of transactions. A frequent mistake is sending Bitcoin to an incorrect address, which, due to the irreversible nature of blockchain transactions, often results in the permanent loss of funds. Double-checking addresses before confirming transactions is crucial.

Scams and phishing attacks are also prevalent in the cryptocurrency space. Users should be wary of unsolicited messages, suspicious offers, and too-good-to-be-true investment opportunities. Verifying the authenticity of websites and communication is essential to avoid falling victim to such schemes.

Technical mistakes, such as confusing Bitcoin with other cryptocurrencies or misunderstanding transaction fees, can also lead to complications.

Educating oneself about the specific requirements and characteristics of Bitcoin transactions is key to avoiding these errors.

Advanced Features

Beyond the basics, Bitcoin offers advanced features that cater to more sophisticated needs and enhance the transactional experience. Multisig wallets, which require multiple signatures to authorize a transaction, provide an added layer of security and are ideal for collaborative financial management, such as in partnerships or organizations.

The Lightning Network represents a significant advancement in Bitcoin's scalability, enabling faster and more cost-effective transactions. By facilitating off-chain transactions that are later settled on the blockchain, the Lightning Network alleviates congestion and reduces transaction fees, making Bitcoin more viable for microtransactions and everyday purchases.

Atomic swaps are another innovative feature, allowing for the trustless exchange of different cryptocurrencies without the need for a centralized intermediary. This enhances the interoperability and flexibility of cryptocurrency transactions, paving the way for more integrated and efficient digital asset ecosystems.

These advanced features underscore Bitcoin's adaptability and the ongoing innovation within the cryptocurrency space, offering users a broad spectrum of options for managing and transacting in Bitcoin according to their specific needs and preferences.

Investing in Bitcoin

This chapter delves into the heart of Bitcoin investing, unraveling the layers of risk and reward that define this modern financial odyssey. As we embark on this journey, our quest is not merely to understand Bitcoin as a digital currency but to grasp its profound implications on the landscape of investment.

The Genesis of a Digital Revolution

Bitcoin, born from the crucible of the 2008 financial crisis, was conceived as an antidote to the vulnerabilities of traditional financial systems. Its decentralized nature, underpinned by blockchain technology, offers a stark contrast to the centralized edifices of banks and financial institutions. This foundational difference is not just technical; it's philosophical, promising a future where financial sovereignty is returned to the individual.

The Investment Odyssey

Bitcoin's appeal as an investment asset lies in its multifaceted nature. It is at once a store of value, likened to digital gold, and a speculative asset, with the potential for significant returns. This duality is both its allure and its challenge. The decentralized ledger not only ensures transparency and security but also introduces a new paradigm of scarcity in the digital world, with a capped supply of 21 million bitcoins.

Navigating the Chapter

This chapter aims to be your compass in the often-turbulent seas of Bitcoin investing. We will first chart the waters of risk, understanding the tempests that can unsettle even the sturdiest of investment vessels. From the whirlpools of market volatility to the unpredictable winds of regulatory change, we prepare you to navigate these challenges with insight and fortitude.

In counterbalance, we will explore the islands of reward that beckon the intrepid investor. The promise of unprecedented returns, the allure of an asset unbound by inflationary chains, and the horizon of a technology that is reshaping the financial world.

With the map laid before us, we will then delve into the art of navigation. Bitcoin trading strategies will be our stars, guiding us through the night, offering paths illuminated by technical analysis and fundamental insights. Whether you're setting sail for the long voyage of investment or navigating the swift currents of trading, this chapter aims to be your beacon.

In the dichotomy of long-term versus short-term investment, we find our balance. The steady gaze of the long-term investor contrasts with the agile reflexes of the short-term trader. Each approach, with its merits and perils, offers a unique perspective on Bitcoin investing.

The Risks and Rewards of Bitcoin Investing

In the realm of Bitcoin investing, the interplay of risk and reward shapes the contours of the investment landscape. This section delves into the inherent risks that accompany the allure of Bitcoin, juxtaposed against the compelling rewards that have drawn investors to this digital frontier.

Risks of Bitcoin Investing

Market Volatility

The seas of Bitcoin are known for their turbulent waves, with price fluctuations that can be both swift and steep. This volatility is a hallmark of Bitcoin's investment profile, driven by factors such as market sentiment, liquidity levels, and significant news events. Unlike traditional assets, Bitcoin operates in a relatively nascent market, where the interplay of supply and demand can lead to pronounced price movements. Investors must navigate these waters with caution, understanding that the potential for rapid gains is mirrored by the risk of equally swift declines.

Regulatory Uncertainty

The regulatory landscape for Bitcoin is a mosaic of global perspectives, with some nations embracing the digital currency, while others cast a wary eye. This patchwork of regulations introduces a layer of uncertainty that can impact Bitcoin's value and legality. Changes in regulatory stance, such as the imposition of bans or stringent regulations in key markets, can trigger volatility and affect investor confidence. Navigating this uncertain terrain requires a vigilant eye on global regulatory developments, as they can significantly influence the investment climate for Bitcoin.

Security Concerns

The digital realm of Bitcoin, while offering unprecedented opportunities, also harbours unique risks. The spectre of hacking looms large, with instances of exchange breaches and stolen funds serving as stark reminders of the security challenges. Beyond external threats, investors must contend with the risks of fraud and the potential loss of private keys. The loss of these cryptographic keys, akin to losing the combination to a digital vault, can result in the irrevocable loss of Bitcoin holdings. Vigilance and robust security measures are the bulwarks against these digital perils.

Adoption and Technology Risks

The promise of Bitcoin hinges on its widespread adoption and technological resilience. However, these are not guaranteed outcomes. The journey towards mass adoption is fraught with obstacles, from scalability challenges to competition from other cryptocurrencies and emerging technologies. Should Bitcoin falter in its bid for widespread use, or should significant technological vulnerabilities emerge, the investment proposition could be undermined. Investors must weigh these adoption and technology risks against the potential rewards, recognizing that the path to digital currency ubiquity is neither straight nor assured.

Rewards of Bitcoin Investing

High Return Potential

Amidst the risks, the lure of significant returns stands as a beacon for investors. Bitcoin's historical performance has been marked by meteoric rises, capturing the imagination of investors seeking outsized gains. While past performance is not indicative of future results, the potential for substantial returns remains a compelling aspect of Bitcoin's investment appeal. This high return potential is underpinned by Bitcoin's capped supply and growing demand, particularly in an era of digital transformation.

Inflation Hedge

In an age where fiat currencies are vulnerable to inflation, Bitcoin presents itself as digital gold, a hedge against the erosion of purchasing power. Its fixed supply contrasts with the expandable nature of fiat currencies, offering a safeguard against inflationary pressures. This proposition has gained traction in times of economic uncertainty, positioning Bitcoin as a potential store of value for investors seeking refuge from inflationary tides.

Increasing Adoption

The tapestry of Bitcoin adoption is being woven with increasing threads, from businesses integrating Bitcoin payments to financial institutions exploring Bitcoin investments. This growing acceptance enhances Bitcoin's legitimacy and utility, bolstering its investment case. As adoption widens, from retail to institutional investors, the foundation for Bitcoin's value proposition strengthens, offering a compelling narrative for investment.

Decentralization and Transparency

At the heart of Bitcoin lies the ethos of decentralization and transparency, enabled by blockchain technology. This framework offers a departure from traditional financial systems, with their opaque operations and central points of control. The transparency of Bitcoin's ledger and the decentralization of its network not only enhance security but also imbue Bitcoin with intrinsic qualities that are valued in an increasingly interconnected and scrutinized financial landscape.

In the balance of risks and rewards, Bitcoin investing presents a narrative of contrast. The potential for significant returns and the allure of a decentralized, transparent digital currency are juxtaposed against the realities of market volatility, regulatory uncertainty, and security challenges. As investors chart their course in the Bitcoin realm, this dichotomy serves as a guiding light, illuminating the path between caution and opportunity.

Bitcoin Trading Strategies

Navigating the Bitcoin market demands a blend of insight and strategy, where the confluence of fundamental and technical analysis lights the path. This section dissects these analytical frameworks, offering a compass for those seeking to chart their course through the volatile waters of Bitcoin trading.

Fundamental Analysis

Market Sentiment

The pulse of the market, sentiment wields the power to sway Bitcoin's price with the force of collective emotion. This ephemeral yet potent force can be gauged through various channels, from social media buzz to investor surveys, painting a picture of the market's mood. Positive sentiment, driven by bullish news or breakthroughs, can propel prices skyward, while fear and uncertainty can plunge them into the depths. Navigating this landscape requires a keen sense of the market's heartbeat, interpreting signals amidst the noise to anticipate sentiment-driven movements.

Regulatory News

In the realm of Bitcoin, the pen of the regulator can be mightier than the market's sword. Regulatory announcements, ranging from policy shifts to legal frameworks, can significantly impact Bitcoin's market dynamics. A favorable stance by key nations can legitimize and buoy the market, while stringent regulations can cast shadows of doubt. Savvy traders keep a vigilant watch on the regulatory horizon, deciphering the implications of legal developments and positioning their strategies in anticipation of their market impact.

Technological Developments

At Bitcoin's core lies a tapestry of technology, where innovations and advancements can catalyze shifts in value. From scalability solutions like the Lightning Network to privacy enhancements and interoperability breakthroughs, technological evolution is a cornerstone of Bitcoin's investment narrative. Traders attuned to these developments can glean insights into Bitcoin's future trajectory, understanding that technological milestones not only enhance utility but can also serve as harbingers of market movement.

Technical Analysis

Chart Patterns and Trends

The language of the markets is etched in charts, where patterns and trends whisper the stories of supply and demand. Recognizing these formations, from the bullish optimism of ascending triangles to the cautionary tales of head and shoulders patterns, offers a lens into market sentiment and potential movements. Mastery of chart patterns empowers traders to navigate the market with a map of historical precedents, interpreting the ebb and flow of prices through the geometry of market psychology.

Volume Analysis

The chorus of the market is sung in volumes, where the magnitude of trading speaks volumes about the strength of price movements. An uptrend accompanied by rising volumes can

affirm the conviction behind a rally, while
dwindling volumes may signal a weakening
trend. Volume analysis serves as a beacon,
guiding traders through the fog of market
ambiguity, offering clues to the sustainability of
trends and the potency of price changes.

Indicators and Oscillators

In the toolkit of the technical trader lie the
instruments of precision—indicators and
oscillators. Moving averages smooth the jagged
edges of price movements, revealing underlying
trends amidst the market's tumult. The Relative
Strength Index (RSI) and Moving Average
Convergence Divergence (MACD) oscillate
between the poles of market momentum,
offering insights into overbought or oversold
conditions. These tools, wielded with acumen,
enable traders to dissect market dynamics,
timing their maneuvers with the precision of
seasoned navigators.

In the confluence of fundamental and technical
analysis, traders find their bearings, steering
through the currents of market sentiment,
regulatory winds, and technological tides. The

charts serve as their starlit sky, where patterns and volumes illuminate the path ahead, and indicators act as compasses, guiding towards informed trading decisions. In this intricate dance of analysis, the successful trader harmonizes the rhythm of fundamentals with the melody of technicals, composing a strategy that resonates with the market's ever-changing tune.

Long-Term vs Short-Term Investment in Bitcoin

The journey of Bitcoin investment unfolds along the timelines of intention, where long-term horizons meet short-term ventures. This section delves into the strategic dichotomy, exploring the steadfast patience of long-term investment against the swift agility of short-term trading.

Long-Term Investment in Bitcoin

Buy and Hold Strategy

The essence of the buy and hold strategy lies in its simplicity and profound belief in Bitcoin's long-term trajectory. This approach is anchored in the historical appreciation of Bitcoin, viewing its tumultuous yet upward journey as a testament to its enduring value. Investors adopting this stance are not swayed by the siren songs of market volatility; instead, they see beyond the crests and troughs to a horizon where Bitcoin's fundamental attributes—scarcity, decentralization, and utility—forge a store of value for the digital age. The rationale for holding Bitcoin long-term is not merely speculative; it is a vote of confidence in the transformative potential of this digital asset.

Diversification

Integrating Bitcoin into a diversified portfolio brings the benefits of low correlation with traditional assets, offering a hedge against market downturns and inflationary pressures. This diversification strategy leverages Bitcoin's unique market dynamics to enhance portfolio growth and manage risk, acknowledging that the digital currency's volatility, while pronounced, is a source of potential reward when tempered by the stabilizing influence of other asset classes.

Staking and Interest

For the long-term Bitcoin holder, the journey extends beyond mere appreciation. The avenues of staking and interest accounts open paths to passive income, turning the act of holding into an active investment. Through various platforms and financial instruments, Bitcoin investors can earn returns on their holdings, compounding their growth over time. This strategy not only maximizes the potential of long-term investment but also aligns with the evolving ecosystem of decentralized finance (DeFi), where Bitcoin's utility and liquidity contribute to broader financial innovation.

Short-Term Investment in Bitcoin

Day Trading

Day traders ride the waves of short-term price movements, employing a plethora of strategies—from technical analysis to algorithmic trading—to capitalize on intraday volatility. This approach demands a keen understanding of market dynamics, a disciplined risk management framework, and an unwavering emotional equilibrium. In the fast-paced theater of day trading, each day is a microcosm of possibilities, where meticulous strategy and precise execution can harvest the day's volatile bounty.

Swing Trading

Swing trading occupies the middle ground between the marathon of long-term holding and the sprint of day trading. This strategy is predicated on capturing the gains from market 'swings' or cycles, which may unfold over days to weeks. Swing traders harness technical analysis and market sentiment to identify potential entry and exit points, riding the momentum of trends for short to medium-term gains. This approach requires a blend of patience and agility, as traders must discern the opportune moments to enter the market and when to retreat, capitalizing on the rhythmic pulsations of Bitcoin's price movements.

Arbitrage

In the interstitial spaces of market inefficiencies, arbitrageurs find their niche, exploiting the price differentials across various exchanges. Bitcoin's global market, with its multitude of trading platforms, presents opportunities for quick profits by purchasing Bitcoin on one exchange where the price is lower and selling it on another where the price is higher. This strategy, while seemingly straightforward, demands a high degree of precision, speed, and an understanding of transaction fees and latency, as the windows for arbitrage can be fleeting and narrow.

The divergent paths of long-term and short-term Bitcoin investment reflect the multifaceted nature of this digital asset. Whether anchored in the conviction of Bitcoin's enduring value or navigating the rapid currents of market fluctuations, investors find in Bitcoin a canvas broad and diverse. Each strategy, with its own set of principles and practices, contributes to the dynamic narrative of Bitcoin investing, where the horizons of opportunity are as vast as the depth of strategic thought.

At the heart of our journey lies the recognition that Bitcoin, with its pioneering technology and unique market dynamics, presents a new frontier in the investment world.

The volatility of Bitcoin's market, while daunting, is matched by the potential for significant returns, positioning it as both a speculative asset and a digital store of value. We've delved into the critical importance of staying abreast of regulatory changes, technological advancements, and market sentiment, all of which play pivotal roles in shaping Bitcoin's investment landscape.

Our exploration of trading strategies illuminated the paths of fundamental and technical analysis, each offering tools to decipher the market's language. Whether through the steady gaze of long-term investment or the agile maneuvers of short-term trading, the strategies we've discussed serve as compasses in the vast sea of Bitcoin investing.

As we conclude this chapter, the imperative of informed decision-making and robust risk management stands clear. The journey of Bitcoin investing is not for the faint-hearted but for those armed with knowledge, strategy, and a balanced perspective.

Let this chapter not be an end but a beacon encouraging continued learning and exploration. As the landscape of Bitcoin and cryptocurrency evolves, so too should our understanding and approaches. In the realm of Bitcoin investing, the fusion of patience, insight, and adaptability paves the way for navigating the complexities and capitalizing on the opportunities that lie in the digital age of finance.

The Future of Bitcoin

Upcoming Trends in Cryptocurrency

Next-Generation Blockchain Technologies:
The narrative begins by exploring the frontier of blockchain evolution. Here, advancements are not just incremental; they are revolutionary. Scalability solutions such as Lightning Network and Layer 2 protocols are redefining transaction speeds and efficiency, making Bitcoin more accessible and usable for everyday transactions. Security enhancements, fortified by cutting-edge cryptographic methods, promise an impenetrable fortress safeguarding digital assets against burgeoning cyber threats. Furthermore, the surge in sustainable blockchain solutions addresses the critical environmental concerns, heralding an era where Bitcoin not only thrives in digital realms but also contributes positively to our physical world.

Decentralized Finance (DeFi) Integration:
As the journey continues, we delve into the dynamic world of DeFi, where traditional financial boundaries are dismantled, and innovative financial services emerge. Bitcoin's

integration into DeFi platforms is a confluence of heritage and innovation, melding Bitcoin's robust security and scarcity with the versatility and adaptability of DeFi ecosystems. This fusion is transforming financial services, from lending and borrowing to insurance and derivatives, making them more inclusive, transparent, and efficient. Bitcoin, within DeFi, is not just a currency; it's a foundational asset driving a financial revolution.

Bitcoin and Non-Fungible Tokens (NFTs):
The exploration then shifts to the vibrant intersection of Bitcoin and NFTs. This convergence is birthing new forms of digital ownership and artistry, where Bitcoin's indelible ledger becomes a canvas for unique digital creations. NFTs on Bitcoin platforms, such as those enabled by protocols like RGB, are opening up new avenues for creators and collectors, blending the realms of art, culture, and technology. This segment showcases how Bitcoin, an architect of financial change, also becomes a patron of digital artistry and innovation.

Quantum Computing's Potential Impact:

The final stretch of our exploration casts light on the shadow of quantum computing, a formidable force with the potential to redefine cryptographic security. This segment navigates the complexities of quantum algorithms and their potential to challenge the cryptographic bedrock of Bitcoin and other cryptocurrencies. Yet, in this challenge lies an opportunity for evolution, driving the cryptocurrency community towards quantum-resistant cryptographic techniques. This proactive adaptation underscores the resilience and forward-thinking ethos of the cryptocurrency ecosystem, ensuring that Bitcoin and its brethren are prepared to weather the quantum storm.

Regulatory Landscape for Bitcoin

Navigating Current Regulatory Frameworks: The exploration begins with a panoramic view of the regulatory frameworks in key markets across the globe. From the stringent scrutiny of the SEC in the United States to the progressive stance of Japan's Financial Services Agency, these regulatory bodies play a pivotal role in shaping Bitcoin's adoption and integration into mainstream financial systems. The narrative uncovers how regulations, while aimed at ensuring security and combating illicit activities, also serve as a litmus test for Bitcoin's resilience and adaptability. This section elucidates the ripple effects of these regulations on investor confidence, market stability, and innovation within the Bitcoin ecosystem.

Balancing Act: Innovation and Consumer Protection:

As the journey progresses, we delve into the heart of regulatory challenges—striking a harmonious balance between fostering innovation and ensuring consumer protection. This segment highlights the tightrope walk regulators must perform, where overly stringent regulations may stifle growth and innovation, while lax policies could leave consumers vulnerable to fraud and market manipulations. Through illustrative examples and case studies, this discourse brings to light the nuanced approaches adopted by various jurisdictions, aiming to nurture the revolutionary potential of Bitcoin while erecting safeguards against its potential pitfalls.

The Dialogue of Development: Policymakers and the Crypto Community:

At the core of regulatory evolution lies the dynamic dialogue between policymakers and the cryptocurrency community. This part of the narrative emphasizes the importance of collaborative regulation, where open communication and mutual understanding pave the way for policies that support sustainable growth. It showcases instances of regulatory sandboxes and public consultations as crucibles for crafting regulations that resonate with the needs of both the market and its participants. This dialogue is not just about finding common ground; it's about building a foundation for innovation that is robust, inclusive, and forward-looking.

Speculating on Future Regulatory Trends:

As the segment approaches its culmination, it ventures into the realm of speculation, casting an eye towards the horizon of regulatory trends. Here, the discourse explores potential shifts towards global regulatory harmonization, where cross-border cooperation could lead to standardized regulations that facilitate international trade and investment in Bitcoin. The narrative also contemplates the emergence of decentralized regulatory technologies (RegTech) and their role in automating compliance and enhancing transparency. This forward-looking speculation not only illuminates the path ahead but also invites readers to ponder the role they might play in shaping this future landscape.

Bitcoin's Place in the Future Economy

Bitcoin's Multifaceted Economic Role:
Our journey begins by examining Bitcoin's evolving identity as a store of value, a medium of exchange, and a unit of account. In tumultuous economic times, Bitcoin emerges as a digital bastion of value, akin to gold, attracting individuals and institutions alike seeking refuge from inflationary pressures. As a medium of exchange, Bitcoin's potential is increasingly realized, with advancements in scalability and adoption paving the way for its use in daily transactions, transcending borders and bureaucratic constraints. As a unit of account, though nascent, Bitcoin's journey is marked by a

growing acceptance within niche markets and communities, heralding a future where it could become a standard measure of economic value.

Enhancing Financial Inclusion:
The narrative then shifts to Bitcoin's transformative potential in bridging the vast chasm of financial exclusion. For the unbanked and underbanked, Bitcoin offers a beacon of hope, providing access to global financial services without the need for traditional banking infrastructure. This section highlights real-world examples and stories of empowerment, where Bitcoin has facilitated remittances, savings, and entrepreneurship among those previously marginalized by the conventional financial system. Through Bitcoin, financial inclusion is not just an ideal; it's becoming a tangible reality for millions worldwide.

Integration and Coexistence with Traditional Finance:
As we venture further, the discussion pivots to Bitcoin's integration into the traditional financial ecosystem and its symbiotic relationship with central bank digital currencies (CBDCs). This

segment uncovers the evolving landscape where Bitcoin and traditional financial institutions are finding common ground, from investment portfolios incorporating Bitcoin as an asset class to banks offering cryptocurrency custody services. The emergence of CBDCs presents a nuanced dialogue, where Bitcoin's decentralized ethos contrasts with state-backed digital currencies, yet together, they redefine the contours of monetary sovereignty and financial autonomy.

Philosophical Reflections on Bitcoin's Essence:

In the concluding reflections, the discourse transcends the economic and delves into the philosophical underpinnings of Bitcoin. Bitcoin is more than a currency; it's a manifestation of a growing discourse on the nature of money, sovereignty, and individual freedom in the digital era. This section contemplates Bitcoin's role in challenging traditional monetary paradigms, fostering a global conversation on financial privacy, autonomy, and the decentralization of power. Through Bitcoin, we are not merely witnessing the evolution of currency but a profound shift in the societal ethos towards a more open, equitable, and decentralized world.

In this closing segment, Bitcoin is envisioned not just as a participant in the future economy but as a catalyst for a broader transformation. Its journey from a novel digital asset to a pivotal economic force encapsulates a broader narrative of innovation, inclusion, and introspection. As we peer into the horizon, Bitcoin's place in the future economy appears not just promising but pivotal, heralding a new chapter in the annals of economic history where technology, philosophy, and humanity converge.

Getting Started with Bitcoin

Step-by-step Guide to Your First Bitcoin

1. Understanding Bitcoin: Before diving into the world of Bitcoin, it's crucial to have a solid understanding of what it is, how it works, and the principles behind it. Spend time researching and learning about Bitcoin, its history, and the technology that underpins it, blockchain.

2. Setting Up a Wallet: Your first step in acquiring Bitcoin is to set up a digital wallet. Wallets come in various forms, including software wallets (desktop, mobile, and online) and hardware wallets. Each type has its advantages and considerations regarding security, convenience, and control.

Software Wallets: Ideal for beginners and those who want easy access to their Bitcoin. They're typically free and easy to set up but vary in security features.

Hardware Wallets: Offer the highest security for storing Bitcoin. They store your private keys offline, making them immune to online hacking attempts. However, they can be more complex for beginners and come with a cost.

3. Purchasing Bitcoin:

Cryptocurrency Exchanges: Sign up for an account with a reputable cryptocurrency exchange where you can buy Bitcoin using fiat currencies (e.g., USD, EUR) or other cryptocurrencies.

Bitcoin ATMs: Bitcoin ATMs allow you to buy Bitcoin with cash. They're a quick and straightforward way to purchase small amounts of Bitcoin, though fees can be higher than online exchanges.

Peer-to-Peer Platforms: Allows you to buy Bitcoin directly from other people. This can be a way to get Bitcoin at competitive rates, but be cautious of fraud and always use a platform that offers escrow services.

4. Conducting Your First Transaction: Once you have Bitcoin in your wallet, you can start using it for transactions. Whether you're buying goods or services online or sending Bitcoin to someone

else, the process typically involves entering the recipient's address, specifying the amount, and confirming the transaction. Transactions are irreversible, so double-check the details before confirming.

5. Managing and Securing Your Bitcoin:
Understanding how to manage and secure your Bitcoin is crucial. Keep your software updated, consider using multi-signature wallets for additional security, and never share your private keys with anyone.

Resources for Further Learning

1. Official Bitcoin Resources:
Bitcoin.org: Offers a wide range of guides, tutorials, and information for both beginners and advanced users.

Bitcoin Whitepaper: Reading the original whitepaper by Satoshi Nakamoto provides fundamental insights into Bitcoin's purpose and design.

2. Online Courses and Tutorials:

Platforms like Coursera, Udemy, and Khan Academy offer comprehensive courses on Bitcoin and blockchain technology, ranging from beginner to advanced levels. These courses are often taught by industry experts and provide a structured learning path.

3. Books:

"The Bitcoin Standard" by Saifedean Ammous: Provides a historical context of money and how Bitcoin fits into the evolution of financial systems.

"Mastering Bitcoin" by Andreas M. Antonopoulos: A technical guide that explains how Bitcoin works under the hood, suitable for those with a technical background.

4. Podcasts and YouTube Channels:

Podcasts like "The Pomp Podcast" and "Unchained" regularly feature interviews with cryptocurrency experts and discussions on the latest trends and developments in the Bitcoin space.

YouTube channels such as Andreas M. Antonopoulos and aantonop offer in-depth explanations and discussions on various Bitcoin topics.

5. Cryptocurrency Forums and Communities:

Engaging with the community can provide real-time insights and help. Platforms like BitcoinTalk Forum, Reddit's r/Bitcoin, and Cryptocurrency subreddits are valuable resources for advice, discussions, and staying updated on news.

6. Conferences and Meetups:

Attending Bitcoin and blockchain conferences, workshops, and meetups can be an excellent way to learn from experts, network with other Bitcoin enthusiasts, and stay informed about the latest industry trends.

Diving into Bitcoin can be a rewarding journey, offering insights into a potentially transformative technology. By starting with a solid foundation and continually seeking knowledge, you'll be well-equipped to navigate the exciting world of Bitcoin.

Conclusion

As we reach the end of our journey through the world of Bitcoin, it's clear that what began as an experimental digital currency has evolved into a significant global financial phenomenon. From its humble origins to becoming a symbol of financial innovation, Bitcoin challenges traditional monetary systems and offers a glimpse into a future where decentralization and digital currencies play a central role.

Bitcoin's journey is far from over; it continues to evolve, adapt, and inspire a wave of new technologies and cryptocurrencies. Its underlying principles of decentralization, transparency, and security are shaping not just finance but various sectors, promising a more equitable and efficient world.

As you close this book, remember that your exploration of Bitcoin doesn't end here. The landscape is rapidly changing, with new developments, challenges, and opportunities emerging all the time. Staying informed, curious, and engaged with the community will enrich your understanding and experience with Bitcoin.

Thank You

I extend my heartfelt gratitude to you, the reader, for embarking on this journey through the intricacies of Bitcoin. Your willingness to explore this groundbreaking technology speaks volumes about your openness to new ideas and your desire to understand the forces shaping our financial future. Thank you for your time, attention, and eagerness to learn.

Call to Action

Now, armed with knowledge and insights about Bitcoin, I encourage you to take the next steps:

Engage: Join Bitcoin forums, social media groups, or local meetups to connect with like-minded individuals. The community is Bitcoin's backbone, offering support, knowledge, and camaraderie.

Experiment: Consider setting up your own Bitcoin wallet and conducting small transactions to familiarize yourself with the process. Hands-on experience is invaluable.

Educate: Share your knowledge with others. Whether it's discussing Bitcoin with friends or writing about your experiences, spreading awareness contributes to a more informed and open-minded society.

Stay Informed: The world of Bitcoin is ever-evolving. Keep learning, stay updated on the latest news, and continue to explore the broader implications of blockchain technology.

In the spirit of Bitcoin's decentralized ethos, every individual's participation strengthens the network. Your journey into Bitcoin, whether as a user, investor, advocate, or innovator, contributes to the ongoing narrative of this revolutionary digital currency. Together, we stand at the forefront of a financial renaissance, poised to embrace the endless possibilities that Bitcoin and blockchain technology have to offer.

Alex Knight

Disclaimer

This book is intended to provide general
information regarding Bitcoin and its associated
technologies. The contents of this book,
including but not limited to text, graphics,
images, and other material, are for informational
purposes only and not intended as financial
advice, legal advice, or any other type of
professional advice.

While the author has made every effort to ensure
the accuracy and completeness of the
information contained in this book, the rapidly
evolving nature of Bitcoin and blockchain
technology means that changes can occur
quickly. Therefore, the author does not
guarantee the timeliness, accuracy, or
applicability of any content and expressly
disclaims all liability for errors and omissions in
the content.

The author is not a financial advisor, and this
book should not be used as a basis for making
investment decisions. Before making any
financial decisions, readers are advised to

consult with a qualified professional, especially concerning their specific financial situation.

The views expressed in this book are those of the author and do not necessarily reflect the official policy or position of any other agency, organization, employer, or company. The mention of any specific products, services, or organizations is for informational purposes only and does not constitute an endorsement or recommendation.

Investing in Bitcoin and other cryptocurrencies involves a high level of risk, and there is always the potential of losing money when you invest in cryptocurrencies. Past performance is not indicative of future results. Make sure to consider your investment objectives and consult with a financial advisor if you require professional advice.

By reading this book, you acknowledge and agree that the author and publisher are not liable for any losses or damages that may result from your use of the information contained within this book.